IRON AND STEEL RIDE THE WAVES

By: Mustafa Nejem

TABLE OF CONTENT

Chapter 1

SHIPS BEFORE STEEL

The history of ships and shipbuilding is a long and detailed one. From nearly the earliest civilisations, people have built crafts to facilitate waterborne travel. The first civilisations thrived along rivers – in China along the Yangtze, in India along the Indus, in Egypt along the Nile, and in Mesopotamia at the confluence of the Tigris and Euphrates – and people living along those rivers soon found means of crossing them and travelling up and down them, by using wood and other materials to make boats, of all shapes and sizes. They used boats to move themselves and their goods, animals, and weapons from place to place faster than

they could travel on land. The list of other necessary materials in those early days was quite small: ropes, nails, and a few other small items.

The ancient Mesopotamians used reeds, and the ancient Egyptians used papyrus. Some ancient people even used a form of paper as a basis for constructing a boat. However, wood was the primary material of choice for most maritime civilisations. Common forms of wooden boats in those early days were rafts and dugouts, the former a collection of wooden splints held together in some form or fashion and the latter a large piece of wood with a bit missing whereby the pilot could sit and steer.

Although the common perception of a purpose-built raft perpetuated by fiction stories in which people are shipwrecked and build their own, making criss-cross layers of splints, the earliest rafts were one layer only, a collection of wooden bits just large enough to carry a few people and a few things and held together by whatever was to hand to do the task. Also, people who carved dugouts did so to carry one or a few people. Such early waterborne craft, too, needed something else to propel it along. Early people used poles and paddles (and such practice continued well into the latter centuries as American and European civilisations used canals for trade and

transportation).

One hugely early innovation was the advent of the sail as a means of propulsion. Like many long-ago occurrences, no one knows who built the first sail or if it was purpose-built. Many a sail, early on and into the medieval period, was made of flax or cloth.

The use of a sail allowed those on a boat to go farther faster – provided that the sail had wind to power it, of course. The first sailing ships had one sail. The next innovation was adding a sail; next was the third sail, etc. Larger ships had more than one mast, and naturally, they had more sails. Such advanced construction enabled and emboldened sailors to go farther and farther away from shore, crossing seas like the Mediterranean and North and, eventually, all of the planet's oceans.

A primary motivation for such an increase in potential travel was increased knowledge. Contact with neighbouring towns, villages, peoples, and civilisations led to an exchange of goods, money equivalents, and information. Such contact also led to conflict, as competition for trade routes or the supply of precious goods created tension that often spilt over into warfare of varying degrees. In trade and war, the people or civilisations who could get goods or soldiers farther and faster had a better chance of winning.

Such goals drove the construction of larger and more seaworthy ships. In ancient times, the Greeks built biremes (having two rows of oars) and then triremes (with three rows of oars) and then ever larger numbers of oars on ever larger ships, all carrying soldiers looking to do battle.

The Persian Wars, in which the warring Greek city-states banded together to defeat the invading Persian army not once but twice, featured a number of naval battles, the most famous

of which was the Battle of Salamis, during which the nimbler Greek ships outmanoeuvred the more heavily armed but slower Persian ships and routed them. Such was one innovation, speed, victorious over another, size.

Unable to help themselves, the Greeks turned on one another and fought amongst themselves in the devastating Peloponnesian War, which resulted in nothing so much as an opportunity for other civilisations to take advantage of a sudden Greek weakness. This war, too, featured many naval battles.

The Roman Republic and Empire were well-known for their armies, powered by legions of well-trained and well-armed soldiers. But it was one of Rome's early victories, over Carthage while Rome was still a Republic, that paved the way for domination of much of the known world later on. And to do that, Rome had to become a sea power. It was all good to march armies left, right, and centre in the lands of what is now the Italian peninsula or slightly further afield. But the powerful civilisation of Carthage had a far-flung naval empire and trade network facilitated by a bevy of warships capable of doing great damage. Rome, at least in its earliest stages, had nothing of the kind. The race for Mediterranean hegemony was on.

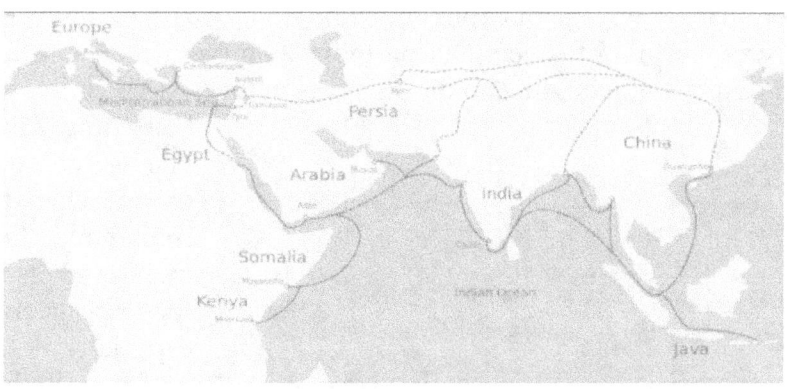

Rome and Carthage slugged it out for decades in three separate wars. The Carthaginian Empire stretched across the Mediterranean, powered by its excellent set of trade and military ships. Rome, at this time, was very much a land-based power. But, as ever, the Romans adapted by capturing and reconstructing a Carthaginian warship. Even the great Carthaginian Hannibal was not enough to subdue Rome despite devastating their armies time after time.

The Romans, riding their naval innovations and finding ways to turn a naval war into a land war, eventually triumphed and claimed primacy in the Mediterranean, a position they would hold for centuries. In the process, they advanced their naval technology and were more than ready for opponents in the future who looked to assert their authority over lands that the Romans considered theirs.

Chinese junks got bigger and bigger as well. The junk dates to Han times, in the 2nd Century B.C., and featured bamboo-spined sails designed for stability and adaptability. As with other early civilisations, the early junk sails were made not of cloth but of grass. Woven fabrics prevailed in the end, however. The more China's influence grew, the bigger the ships got. Perhaps predictably, the junks also featured in the Chinese navy, beginning in the Ming Dynasty, which began in the 14th Century.

During this time, Chinese ships exchanged goods, people, and information along the Silk Road, a network of land and water-based trade routes linking China to Europe via the Middle East.

The most well-known part of the Silk Road was the land-based route, which passed through Central Asia and then to the great port of Constantinople to find other trade routes stretching far and wide to the West. However, many journeys were also considered to have been on the Silk Road, meaning connecting China and points East with what is now Europe and points West were by sea, powered by trade ships sailing along the Asian, African, and European coasts.

As on the Silk Road, only some Chinese expeditions were in pursuit of war. The famous explorer Zheng He headed up the most famous collection of such ships. At the behest of the Yongle Emperor, Zheng He assembled a massive fleet of ships and embarked on a world tour in 1405. About 28,000 soldiers accompanied explorers and traders on nearly 200 ships. It was nominally a voyage of exploration and trade, but the army was there to ensure no conflict. And it was the first of seven. During more than two decades, Zheng He and a varying number of ships and soldiers sailed to distant ports in the South Pacific, the Middle East, and Africa. Also

benefiting from leaps in technology were the people of India, whose ships were known as dhows. They, too, sailed the oceans blue, plying Indian trade far and wide in search of more and more markets and more and more opportunities for expansion. Indian markets would prove especially desirable destinations for European explorers in the late Middle Ages.

European ships got larger, too, with innovations often resulting in a name change: barque, schooner, carrack, and caravel, to name a few. Models of the latter two carried explorers like Vasco Da Gama around the tip of Africa to India and Christopher Columbus across the Atlantic Ocean on a total of four voyages of exploration, determined to "go east by sailing west." In a powerful display of sailing prowess, a handful of carracks carried the Ferdinand Magellan expedition around the world in the early 1520s.

Such explorations served to pique the curiosity of many in Europe, desiring exotic goods from faraway lands. Also, such voyages promise rewards in terms more familiar to those looking for a fight.

The great powers of Europe thought of the New World as a means of improving status, trade, markets, and prestige. Yet the draw of conquest was also powerful. The same Spanish government that sent Columbus and Magellan on voyages of exploration and trade also sent expeditions designed to conquer under the guise of spreading "civilisation". The result was the destruction of many New World indigenous peoples, foremost among them the Aztecs and the Inca, and, further north, the radical Christianization of North American natives who were unfamiliar with European peoples and ways of life. All that exploration and all of that conquest, because the targets were an ocean away, required larger and more powerful ships to transport those explorers and those conquistadors. The shipyards of Europe were quite busy during the Age of Exploration, especially because the risk of losing ships, men, and goods to the caprice of ocean storms and enemy vessels was, in most cases, extraordinarily high.

Chapter 2

CIRCLING THE GLOBE

Ferdinand Magellan was one of many European explorers who yearned for a greater understanding of the world. Of Portuguese origin, he built on the experience of the famed Henry the Navigator and other previous explorers. He was determined to embark on one voyage that would circumnavigate the globe. He did just that – sort of. Magellan's five ships left Spain in September 1519 and encountered several difficulties on their voyage around the world. They recorded a few firsts: It was Magellan who named the Pacific Ocean (from the Latin word for "calm".) It was Magellan's ships that first sailed through the treacherous straits at the southern tip of South America that now bear his name. Storms and other difficulties plagued the voyage – as was the case for nearly every voyage of exploration in those days. Ultimately, the remaining ship returned in September 1522, two weeks shy of three years to the day when it left. Magellan, however, was not on board. He died in a battle on Mactan Island some months before. But he was the voyage commander, and so it is known by his name. His was the first of many.

The Age of Exploration had parallels in an age of warfare among the major European powers, and the thirst for conflict and victory powered innovation in shipbuilding. Europeans built larger and more weaponised ships. Some were familiar models with cannons attached. Others were new models, such as the galleon and the ship of the line, designed exclusively for warfare. Ships of the line and frigates featured most prominently in the naval battles of the Napoleonic Wars. Not to be outdone, the newly independent United States improved on British frigate construction and briefly took the lead in warship production in the early 19th Century.

One type of ship that bridged the gap between commerce and war was the galley, the favoured vessel of pirates from ancient times until well into the 19th Century. This kind of ship is often pictured in adventure story books and movies. People have been building galleys for a long time, but the most common conception in modern times is that of the pirate ship. A comparison of the two is illuminating:

Using wood as the basis for a boat or ship had a few benefits: Wood was relatively cheap, as forests were plentiful. Wood also, for the most part, floated in water, if proportions were right, and so could propel voyages of exploration and war expeditions at a higher speed rate than land-based travel methods. Wood was relatively longer-lasting than the reeds, papyrus, and paper used by earlier civilisations.

Wood had its drawbacks, however. It was particularly susceptible to being ripped open by rocks. Plentiful were the tales of sailors cringing at the sight of rocks looming out of the darkness and the subsequent sound of a hull's tearing open after grazing sharp rocks jutting above the water's surface.

Also, the wooden hull of a ship was often no match for naturally occurring obstacles like barnacles and shipworms, both of which sent many a ship back to port in need of repairs.

For the longest time, repair and avoidance were the only successful strategies employed against such enemies. This changed in the 18th Century with the advent of copper sheathing. Echoing the ancient Greeks, who had bolted lead plates on their hulls now and then, the British Royal Navy attached large copper plates to the underside of many a ship in the mid-1700s. The Government accelerated this practice in the latter half of the century as it fuelled wars worldwide.

It wasn't all war-driven, however. Some merchants in Great Britain and other countries employed copper plating on their hulls to protect their cargo ships. The copper proved an effective shield against the barnacles and shipworms that had bedevilled all-wooden hulls. This copper sheathing was also the first step toward maritime shipping's ultimate innovation: the iron hull.

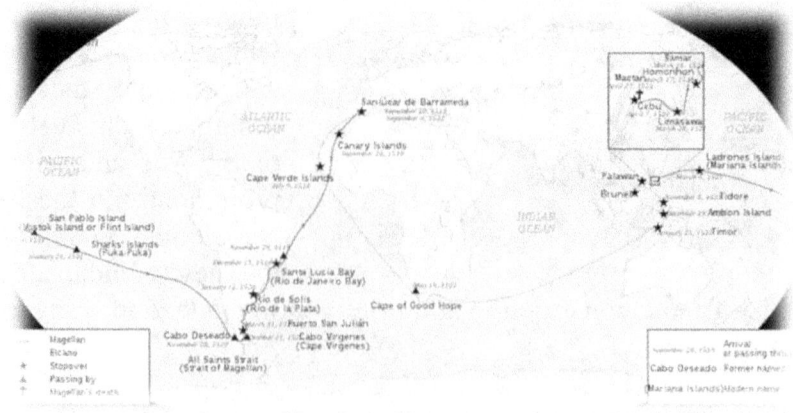

Chapter 3

THE INDUSTRIAL REVOLUTION

Coal formed hundreds of millions of years ago, long before civilisations grew and people began sailing in boats and ships. Plant matter became peat, driven downward by successive generations of greenery. Peat then became lignite, sub-bituminous, bituminous, and anthracite – all types of coal we know today. Each step up the chain creates more carbon in the coal, with anthracite topping out at 86 to 98 per cent carbon.

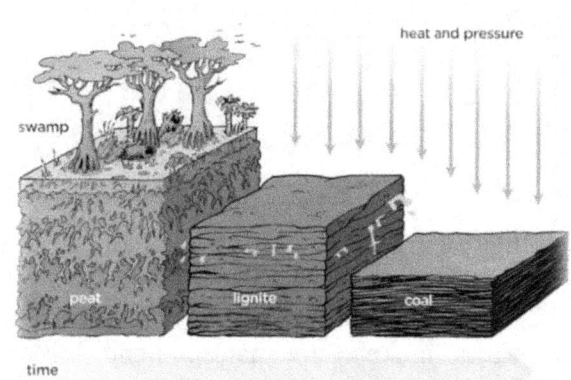

That coal was formed a long, long time ago, but it was only relatively recently – evolutionally speaking – that people started to use coal as a fuel source. Some sources relate mentions by scientists in Ancient Greece. In the 2nd Century A.D., the Romans are known to have used coal in a primitive way. So, too, with the Aztecs several centuries later. Mining of coal in China has been traced to several centuries ago as well; indeed, the famed Venetian explorer Marco Polo mentioned coal being in widespread use during the Yuan Dynasty in the 13th Century. The first systematic use of coal on a larger scale in the West didn't occur until that time in England and Scotland.

Coal is found in beds, often near the surface but more often deep underground. Medieval miners dug shallow pits and used various tools to separate the black-rock coal from other rocks, soil and other materials. Initial methods were rough and left much usable coal in the beds and mines. As technology advanced across the societal spectrum, so did methods of getting coal out of the ground.

A desire to feed and provide for a growing population drove a sustained burst in technology known as the Industrial Revolution, which properly began in the United Kingdom in the 19th Century but had its roots much earlier when it was known as England and then Great Britain. (England absorbed Wales in the 13th Century, and England and Scotland joined in the early 18th Century to form Great Britain. It was in 1800 when Northern Ireland completed the current composite known as the U.K.)

The Industrial Revolution was an explosion of advancement in technology and mechanical processes across a wide spectrum of the population. Many historians say that this series of advancements began in the realm of agriculture with the advent of the seed drill in 1701. A machine was soon doing the work previously done by human hands at a speed far advanced of

the fastest human planter and at a level of efficiency far advanced. Also, at this time, British farmers began to apply a crop rotation system more widely, growing in winter crops that give back nutrients to the soil so spring planting can more readily prosper.

Another of the major industries that underwent major change during the Industrial Revolution was the textile industry. Textiles were many things: clothes, building materials, ship sails. Human hands made all of those things with a modicum of mechanical help. In the 18th Century, a series of inventions transformed the textile industry, driving up outputs to historic levels. With names like Flying Shuttle, Spinning Jenny, and spinning mule, these machines created stronger threads, which would, in turn, make better materials and, in the end, better end products. The final step in the process from human-made to machine-made was the power loom, which entirely automated the spinning and weaving process.

Such machines needed power to drive them. The setup of some machines allowed human power. A very early example of this was the spinning wheel, which could be turned by hand or, in an early innovation, by foot, using a pedal attached at the bottom of the wheel. In this age of industry, however, the emphasis was on power and, significantly, power greater than the human body could produce. The choice for many was the machine, a powerful one. So, the question became how to power such a machine.

The impetus for many of these inventions was time or the saving of it. Determined to produce more things in less time, businessmen spurred their "ideas men" to create machines that could speed up – or, in some cases, replace – human hands.

Such innovations drove an expansion of the population, which created a need for more of everything that a population needed: food, clothing, and shelter. More people living in more homes needed more food and more fuel to heat those homes, and coal became more of a source for home heating.

A byproduct of expanding the number and capacity of furnaces – home and business – burning coal resulted in a stark increase in air pollution. Many large cities during

this time became known as a variant of "The Big Smoke." Burnoff from furnaces was ever-present, inside and out, as some home hearths suffered from inefficiency and smoke getting back inside occasionally. Powerful factories spewed smoke from smokestacks into the air in large quantities. Still, most people determined that such was the price of doing business or keeping warm.

The large increase in work opportunities naturally required a large number of workers. Men, women, and children worked long hours under much (or, in some cases, very little) supervision in spaces large and small, in many cases designed for maximising efficiency and not at all for the comfort of those doing the work. Child labour was quite common at this time, and children of a very young age were known to work very long hours. Laws governing such practices were an afterthought or non-existent. The goal was to do as much as humanly possible in as little time as it took. If that resulted in the injury or death of workers, then employers mourned them but then moved on, hiring more to take the place of those departed.

Such practices were by no means exclusive to factories. Shipbuilding at this time relied on long hours of work done by people who would work their fingers until they were numb and then be compensated meagrely, all in the name of progress they were told was beneficial to all. Dockyards were full of people looking to earn a living by contributing to manual labour.

Several innovations allowed automation to replace human hands, but many processes still required people to perform and run them. This was the case across every industry.

Several advances progressed the practice of coal mining, an industry that saw a huge spike in activity during this time. Increased mining operations employed test bores to better target richer coal supplies. Technological advances allowed deeper drilling, which needed pumps to clear underground water away from the coal. The need to do this provided the impetus for some of the Industrial Revolution's greatest achievements.

At the same time, conditions for workers in such mines were not exemplary. Working at times deep underground, with no little or no light or comfort, men and women and even children toiled in the name of coal harvesting, in the hope that what they were doing was going a way toward helping produce fuel and perhaps heat their homes for them in the process.

Working in such mines was dangerous, as many miners died when they breathed in too many toxic fumes or when mine ceilings and walls collapsed. Still, captains of industry had their goals and targets, and the workers were there to provide the means of meeting them. In this way, a lot has stayed the same since the days of the medieval manor.

To meet the greater demand, coal miners dug deeper and deeper holes in the ground to tap into vast underground reservoirs. The deeper the hole, the more chance for rainwater or aquifer runoff to get into the mine shaft, so mining companies needed a reliable

way of getting the water out. Existing pumps did so much but were insufficient for the need. Thomas Savery, Thomas Newcomen, and James Watt created machines along the way to Watt's eventual powerful steam engine, which could drive the water pumps to do what they were meant to do and enable the mining companies to get even more coal out of the ground.

Chapter 4

IN PURSUIT OF STEAM POWER

Three Englishmen turned their ideas into action in a series of events and results, creating a stepping-stone approach to inventing the most efficient steam engine.

Thomas Savery, operating on either side of the turn of the 18th Century, built a machine to drive water out of the ground to maximise coal production. His machine ran on a pair of steam-powered boilers. It was a start, but it didn't have much power, so that it couldn't have an effect deep in the ground.

Thomas Newcomen came from a different angle: atmospheric pressure. His engine pumped steam into a cylinder, mixed with cold water to produce a vacuum and a consequent amount of atmospheric pressure to power a piston, which drove down and powered the machine. This was a winner, enabling purchase deep in the ground. However, it wastes a lot of energy.

Enter James Watt. Some 50 years after Newcomen's 1711 invention, Watt, working at the University of Glasgow, had his hands on one of Newcomen's machines to repair it. After careful consideration, he identified the source of the wasted energy and then delivered an innovation to stop it: a separate condenser. Newcomen's one condenser had to do double duty, heating up again before it could resume work. Watt's separate condenser kept the water hot and energy from escaping. Significantly, he also made it possible for the machine to work when the piston went up and down. (Newcomen's also wasted the energy potential of the piston going up.) Building on his success, Watt also introduced the now-familiar flywheel and added a centrifugal governor to keep it in its element and control the engine's speed. Watt's new steam engine was a runaway success, soon powering everything it could, including locomotive and ship engines.

The challenge was soon with iron. Long a source of goods, weapons, and transportation devices, iron had a small production scale for much of the time leading up to the Industrial Revolution. The smelting of iron, using a blast

furnace was first known in the days of Han China, in the first two centuries A.D., and then became quite common in the Middle Ages throughout the world.

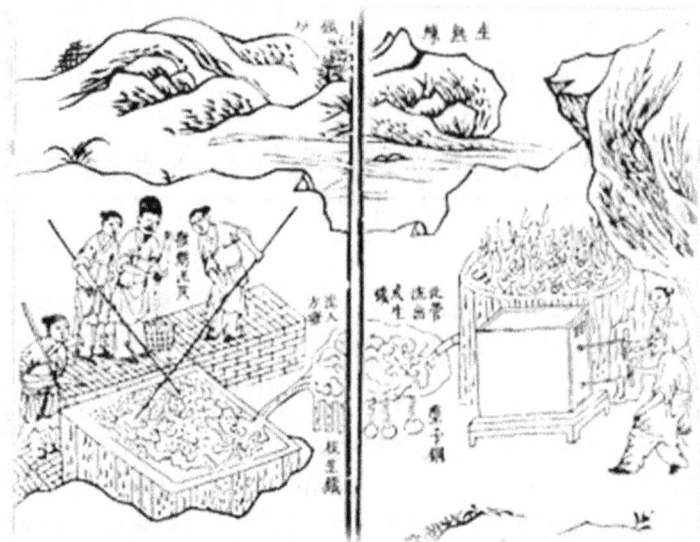

Such was still the production process in the 18th Century when an Englishman named Abraham Darby introduced the coke-fired blast furnace, out of which came cast iron. This innovation spread like wildfire and led to many other fast-paced innovations in machinery, weaponry, and shipbuilding.

Not satisfied, researchers kept tinkering. It was in 1784 that Henry Cort perfected the "puddling" process, whereby iron could be super-heated enough to create wrought iron, which was very stable yet adaptable in terms of use. Soon dotting the landscapes of countries worldwide were iron bridges and, a few decades later, railway lines.

Iron was also an essential element in steam engines. It was nowhere near the first time that inventions and processes coalesced in practice, creating something new and different that became widespread.

It wasn't all steam-powered furnaces in Britain, however. In the early 19th Century, Scotsman John McAdam perfected a new surface for roadways across the U.K. It was so successful that it became associated with its inventor and even named after him: the macadam.

The kingdom had, at this time, as did many other countries, a large system of canals used for transportation of people and goods. Ships of increasing size and capacity regularly tooled up and downstream, powering the national commerce. The production level of the road and canal system combined paled in the face of the ultimate Industrial Revolution innovation: the railroad.

With the ease of use of iron production came the ease of production of iron bars, which were perfect for making railway tracks. The first steam-powered locomotive came along in 1802. Others followed, as did the first public railway, the Stockton and Darlington, in 1825. The construction of railway lines grew exponentially, and tracks and lines soon crisscrossed the country.

Not to be outdone, in the early 19th Century, shipbuilders turned to iron in a big way. It was a few years earlier that the first metal ship appeared. Yorkshire shipbuilders constructed a 12-foot watercraft in 1777. Building on that, a team led by inventor Aaron Manby built an iron-hulled steamer (and named it after himself) that crossed the English Channel in 1822. Three years later, the American inventor John Elgar produced a 60-foot iron-bottomed steamship, *Codorus*, that made a historic river journey between two New York towns.

Much further west (or east), an iron-hulled gunship named *Nemesis,* fitted out by British inventor Jonathan Laird, sailed in defence of operations of the East India Company as early as 1839. Laird again, three years later, crafted the first recognisably sized warship to boast a metal hull, *Guadalupe,* and gave it to the Mexican Navy. Such was the repeated entry of weaponry into the story of the development of ironmaking and shipbuilding. It wasn't long until American shipyards developed a fully ironclad ship. The use of iron in a ship's hull also became increasingly popular in other countries.

In the end, the Industrial Revolution radically changed Western society in a number of ways. First and foremost, the idea of the workplace changed. For aeons, people had worked near where they lived, either on their land or on land owned by others nearby. For much of history, the production of things enforced a rigid social structure whereby those who owned land had wealth and power, and those who didn't own land had to depend on others to meet their fundamental needs. Such was the case long into the Middle Ages and beyond, even as artisans plied their specialist trades and merchants became increasingly wealthier.

The Industrial Revolution resulted in many very large buildings that housed production.

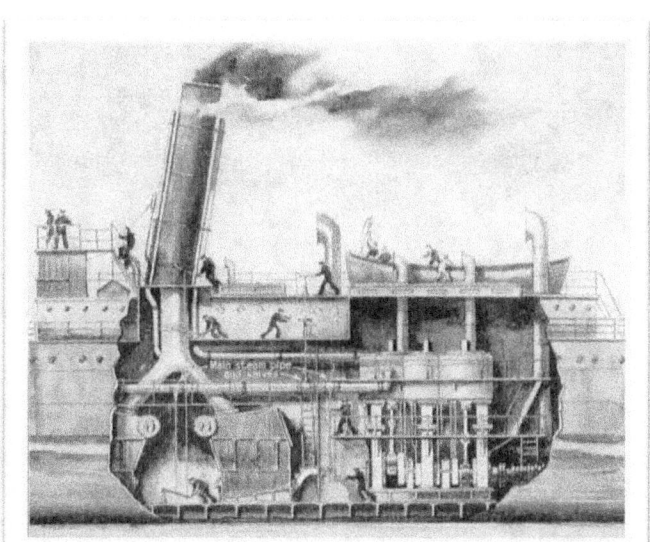

Factories dotted the landscape in many cities and towns, and people travelled to those factories (and out of their homes and neighbourhoods) to work and earn a modicum of wages. Many businesses at this time were small, yet they still offered people a way forward in economic advancement that had not existed before. As had always been the case, the rich grew richer; however, at this time, the poor had the opportunity to grow richer as well, provided that they found a way to save money after spending their meagre wages on food, clothing, and shelter.

Innovation drove the construction of buildings and means of transportation. Railway lines soon connected the corners of continents, offering speedy travel and, in constructing the lines and the locomotives and railway cars, several jobs that had not before been possible. It was the same with the shipbuilding industry. What had always been the case – the opportunity to build bigger and better ships and sporting advancements in technology – was still the case. However, the Industrial Revolution created new opportunities in the maritime realm as well. It wasn't long until watercraft sported new materials and new onboard mechanisms from newly crafted sources. The steam engine, with its flywheel and its increased power capacity, was soon put to good use on ships that sailed ever farther, ever faster.

So, too, was iron used in increasing numbers to protect ship hulls from natural and manmade enemies. But even iron was not enough.

Chapter 5

THE ADVENT OF STEEL

The history of iron production involves a series of innovations designed to increase the capacity and output of metal still found in many places around the globe. In fact, iron is the most commonly found metal on Earth. Intertwined with this series of innovations is the realm of chemistry.

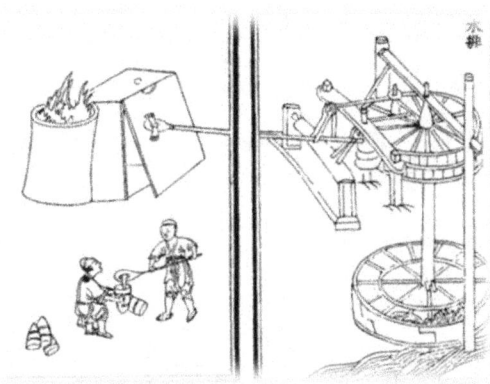

In an effort to improve on the copper alloys that made possible the Bronze Age, enterprising people in Asia in the 2nd Century B.C. perfected the extraction of iron from iron ore by the use of super-heating. The thing needed to do that reliably and relatively safely was a blast furnace, a self-contained apparatus designed to smelt iron to make it into necessary things. The first blast furnaces are known to have been in use in China in the 1st Century A.D. During the smelting process in a blast furnace, iron absorbs another element, carbon, thereby reducing the melting point of iron; that process results in cast iron, which is more easily shaped into needed things. An early form of steel, known as Wootz, was also seen in India in the centuries B.C.

Liquid iron flowed from the furnace onto the floor or ground into channels dug to collect the liquid. Somewhere along the way, someone noticed that the trenches looked like a collection of pigs suckling their mother. Thus, was born the term pig iron.

The producers of liquid iron found that they could pour it into specially constructed moulds to shape it better. In this way, a great many iron tools and weapons. The refined process arose in the West much later than in China in the Middle Ages. By this time, the demand for iron weapons was in full force, and blast furnaces spewed out cannons and guns, workers pouring the pig iron directly into ready-made moulds. Swords were still in demand, of course, and ironmakers produced untold numbers of blades designed to attack and defend at close quarters.

The problem with cast iron, though, metallurgists found, is that the carbon absorbed during the smelting process makes the cast iron brittle and useless for significant shaping. It was all well and good as long as they had moulds; freeform manipulation, however, was rarely possible. The search began for an improvement.

As with the Industrial Revolution, such an improvement came in Britain. Henry Cort, in the mid-19th Century, perfected a Chinese invention, the "puddling" process, which involved workers' using long paddles to stir collections of iron so that oxygen could bond with the carbon, creating carbon dioxide, which was then released, reducing the carbon content of the iron.

Also, at this time came the first hint of steel. The most durable of metals is iron, with very little carbon in it. Primitive forms of steel dot the historical record at various times, including at times B.C. A more recognisable form of steel could be found in the so-called Damascus swords that

were popular during Roman times and into the Middle Ages. But a by-product of the puddling process was a need for even more carbon to be reduced, and a related process, cementation, involved adding powdered charcoal to iron and heating it. A rest period allowed the iron to absorb the carbon in the charcoal, after which more heating produced a more malleable result. The resulting material had what looked like blisters on its surface, and so was called blister steel. This was seen in Britain and Germany in the 1600s and could be readily made into rolled form.

A further innovation came 200 years later in the form of a different need. On the lookout for a way to upgrade the metal in the springs of his products, the British clockmaker Benjamin Huntsman found that iron could be poured into a crucible and then treated to remove the refuse resulting from cementation.

Inefficiency was still a part of the iron and steel production process. As the Industrial Revolution drove advancement, demand for more and more iron – to produce thousands of miles of railway tracks, for example – reached a fever pitch. It was yet another Englishman, Henry Bessemer, who developed an apparatus and a chemical process that solved most of the existing problems.

Building on the idea of a crucible, Bessemer crafted a cylinder that resembled an egg or a pear. Into that cylinder, called a converter, went iron. Then, oxygen was blown into the converter.

As Bessemer knew from earlier innovations, getting the carbon out of the iron was the key, and the addition of oxygen would result in carbon-oxygen bonding and the release of both in the form of carbon dioxide. Bessemer's converter was much better than the earlier version and removed trace elements of silicon found in iron. The converter was also delivered to the speed department. Unfortunately for Bessemer, the process was too fast, removing too much carbon and leaving too much oxygen behind.

Most great inventions are the product of more than one mind and set of hands, so it was with the Bessemer Process. His countryman Robert Mushet was also working in this area and set

about adding another element, manganese, to the mix. Specifically, he used a compound of carbon, iron, and manganese known as spiegeleisen (a German word roughly translated into English as "mirror iron"). Buchet found that his theory was correct and then found the correct quantity of spiegeleisen to employ. He shared his findings with Bessemer, who gladly adopted them into his work. The result was a resounding success, but only after one last step. Henry Bessemer is perhaps most well-known for his steel-making process, revolutionising the industry. However, he also had several other significant achievements.

His father, Anthony, lived in Paris for a time and joined the French Academy of Science. Fleeing the French Revolution, he returned to his homeland and promptly invented a process for making gold chains; his success brought him wealth, and into that wealth, Henry was born.

A scientist and curious mind like his father, Henry also took to inventing, starting with a group of machines that made bronze powder to use in gold paint. The resulting Nuremberg powder made young Henry a lot of money. Growing up in the heady days of the Industrial Revolution, he saw many opportunities for advancement and wealth. Some well-known accidents involving the collapse of iron buildings and bridges in the mid-19th Century spurred many scientists to find a replacement for cast iron. Bessemer was one such who also saw an opportunity to make better weapons to sell to the British Government, which fought its share of wars in the 19th Century.

Building on the work of others, Bessemer made famous his Process for steel production, parlaying its introduction into the construction of steelworks in Sheffield. He was very, very successful.

He also invented many other things, most involving iron and steel and a few involving glass. He also designed a steamship, the SS Bessemer, with a mechanism designed to remain level no matter how high the waves were underneath. The victim of disinterest, it never saw the light of day, even as a working model. At his death in 1898, he held more than 120 patents. He had also achieved a knighthood.

Still not done, Bessemer discovered that another trace element, phosphorous, if found in iron in a high enough quantity, could still make the iron brittle. Yet another element had to be taken out. (At that time, some areas with iron ore had it without phosphorous; such areas were relatively rare.)

It was a Welshman (Sidney Thomas) who put the whole thing over the top, finding that adding limestone removed the phosphorous, making the Bessemer Process safe as a means of producing steel. Bessemer shared his innovation with the world, and steel production (and demand) hit an all-time high.

Still not done, Bessemer discovered that another trace element, phosphorous, if found in iron in a high enough quantity, could still make the iron brittle. Yet another element had to be taken out. (At that time, some areas with iron ore had it without phosphorous; such areas were relatively rare.)

It was a Welshman (Sidney Thomas) who put the whole thing over the top, finding that adding limestone removed the phosphorous, making the Bessemer Process safe as a means of producing steel. Bessemer shared his innovation with the world, and steel production (and demand) hit an all-time high.

Chapter 6

ISAMBARD KINGDOM BRUNEL

The most famous engineer in British history, Isambard Kingdom Brunel, was born to parents with French sympathies in the shadow of war with France. Marc Brunel, his father, was born in France and, as an adult, met Sophia Kingdom, whom he later married. They gave their famous son their names: Marc Brunel's second name was Isambard. Thus, he was named Isambard Kingdom Brunel, born on April 9. 1806, in Portsmouth, Hampshire. He was their third child, after daughters Sophia and Emma.

Marc Brunel had deep ties to France. He was born there, in Normandy, in 1769. He was 20 when the French Revolution began. By then, he served in the French Navy, having had a classical education and done time at a Rouen seminary, where he learned hands-on skills like carpentry and design but showed no interest in becoming a priest. He was back there in 1793, avowing sympathies for the troubled, targeted King Louis XVI, when he met Sophia Kingdom, an Englishwoman working in Rouen as a governess. They pledged fealty to each other just before Brunel fled the country, bound for America.

In New York, Brunel parlayed his skills and charm into a job as Chief Engineer of New York City, then one of the biggest cities in the world. The Industrial Revolution had also begun to take hold in the United States, and demand was high for machines, designs, and know-how. Unbeknownst to Brunel, the love of his life had been arrested as a suspected spy and targeted for the guillotine. Only the fall of the Reign of Terror's chief architect, Maximilien Robespierre, spared Sophia from death. She fled homeward, met there by Brunel, who returned in 1798, having made a name for himself designing houses, docks, and shipyards for a devoted American audience. Brunel and Kingdom married in 1799 and remained in Britain for the rest of their lives.

Brunel put his engineering talents to work again, designing machines for mills and other plants and, in one case, designing an entire sawmill. Adept at lateral thinking, he designed a machine to mass-produce soldiers' boots. His timing was slightly off, as the Napoleonic Wars ended in 1815 before his machine could be fully employed.

By then, young Isambard had followed in his father's footsteps, embarking on a classical education in France and enrolling in a French university at age fourteen. A brilliant child, he showed promise in his knowledge of his subjects and engineering designs. His father and his tutor, the famous French watchmaker and mechanical tinkerer Louis Breguet, encouraged him to think big and draw what he envisioned.

Even though Marc Brunel was successful at designing machines that found much use, such as one to mass-produce ship's pulleys, he was not unlike many of his ilk at that time in that he ran up debts that he could not pay. In 1821, he surrendered to authorities, who threw him in debtors' prison until he could pay the £5,000 that he owed. (In those days, that was quite a bit of money, much more than he could comfortably earn by designing a new machine.)

The shrewd Brunel let it be known that he was thinking of sharing his designs with a foreign power, namely Russian Tsar Alexander I, and it wasn't long before the British Government waived the debt and restored him to civility. This occurred just before his son returned from France.

Isambard, no longer quite young, joined his father as an assistant engineer on a project with bold ambitions: to build a tunnel under the River Thames 75 feet deep. The idea was to link travel from the north bank of the famous river to the south bank without building a bridge over the top. It was a daring proposal with more of its share of sceptics, initially and right through construction. However, the famous Brunel perseverance took hold and guided the proceedings. It was the 20-year-old Isambard's first grand project.

It was a challenging proposition. For a start, the riverbed at the intended south bank location, Rotherhithe, needed to be solid. Marc Brunel had produced a revolutionary design for tunnelling shields a few years earlier and, during this project, employed it to ensure the safety of the workers creating the tunnel. It worked, to a large extent, although it didn't save them from contracting diseases from the sewage-filled water seeping through in small streams.

Employing the shield, the workers carried on through two severe floodings in consecutive years.

Isambard Brunel was injured during the second flood in 1828 and was out of action for months. Six workers died in that second accident.

Sent to Brislington to heal, Brunel heard about a competition to design a new bridge over the River Avon in nearby Bristol. Intrigued and up for a challenge, he submitted a series of designs. Some sources say he eventually won the competition after the head

judge tried to get his design approved, and construction on the still-iconic structure began in 1831. (Although this bridge, the Clifton, is now considered one of Brunel's prime legacies, he did not live to see it finished. Civil unrest not long after construction began resulted in a halt; funds ran out, and production did not resume until three decades later. Still, workers finished the remaining pieces in 1864, and the 700-foot-long bridge remains one of Bristol's most famous sights.)

Meanwhile, construction on the Thames Tunnel continued, still slowly. As was often the case, such projects required a lot of money. Marc Brunel kept having to requisition the Government for more to pay for more labour and more equipment, such as the steam engine that powered the water pump that drained the water runoff from the tunnel-digging operation (another example of the utility of James Watt's ultimate device). In 1835, he employed a new shield, replacing the broken-down old one. A handful of other impediments remained, including flooding, fires, and gas leaks. Finally, in 1841, the tunnel was complete, uniting Rotherhithe with Wapping on the north side of the Thames. The final touches were roadways and lighting. The grand public opening occurred on March 25, 1843. By that time, young Brunel had moved on to other things.

He had somehow found the time to court and marry Elizabeth Horsley in 1836. He was soon on the road again, however, pursuing new projects. One of those was designing what would become London's Paddington Station.

When the Clifton Bridge project stalled, Isambard Brunel found something else to challenge himself. On the back of notoriety for several well-known designs of docks in London and beyond, he was appointed Chief Engineer of the newly formed Great Western Railway. The railroad had well and truly arrived by this time, and Brunel envisioned a passenger's being able to board a train in London, pay once, and then arrive in Bristol, far away. (As it happened, Brunel had even grander plans, envisioning the Great Western *Seaway*, whereby passengers could disembark in Bristol and board a ship bound for America. This vision of transatlantic travel would come to fruition, but not before he cemented his legacy on the rails.)

Railroads were on the upswing at this time. The Industrial Revolution had bequeathed several inventions that made it much easier and cheaper to lay railway tracks, build engines and cars, and then run a train on those tracks. World-leading

Britain was soon joined by other countries, laying track as fast as their technology and economy would allow them.

Meanwhile, Brunel was deep in the weeds with the GWR. He insisted on surveying every inch of the route himself, planning the route meticulously. Not one to shy away from a bold decision, he decreed that the new railroad would operate on a 7 feet ¼ inch-broad track gauge rather than the narrow standard gauge, 4 feet 8½ inches. At the time, other railway lines in Britain, including the first-in-the-country Stockton and Darlington, operated on the standard gauge, as did most other railways worldwide. However, Brunel wanted more speed and greater capacity at that speed and decided on the broad gauge.

In practice, all new locomotives and cars had to be built with wheels the width of the broad gauge. Also, existing engines and cars that ran on the standard gauge would be unable to use the GWR's tracks because of the gauge disparity. It would mean exclusivity on the line, but it would also mean that the new company would have to provide plenty of its stock.

Such was not the concern of the railway's Chief Engineer. Like his father, the younger Brunel proved stubborn once his mind was made up. His trademark stove top hat in place, he would insist that his way was the right way and, chomping on his ever-present cigar, usually get his way.

The new railway path presented new challenges, requiring innovative designs for bridges, stations, and tunnels. Brunel provided them all, working away in his characteristic workaholic fashion, some days putting in 20 hours of toil before sleeping. His designs included one for the Box Tunnel, which, when completed, was the longest railway tunnel in the world, at 1.83 miles.

The tunnel went through Box Hill, near Corsham, between Swindon and Bath. The gradient was a steep 1 in 100. The surrounding material was considered extremely dangerous to construction, but Brunel ploughed ahead, taking all necessary precautions. In the end, the tunnel took three years to finish, by which time workers had used 30 million bricks to line the tunnel walls. It was a triumph of engineering, of manmade tenacity over adversity. It was one of the highlights of the Great Western Railway, which ran its first trains along the line in 1841.

As modern engineer, Chris Wise of Expedition EE Engineering has said, "He took people straight from the medieval to the industrial age as he cut the journey time from London to Bristol from two-and-a-half days to two-and-a-half hours."

Having launched construction of that tunnel, Brunel again turned to something different. He was certainly glad to know that the Box Hill had been completed in 1841, but by then, he was pursuing the crown jewel of his engineering desire, a ship that would sail across the Atlantic Ocean. In 1836 came the Great Western Ship Company, with Brunel's friend and fellow engineer Thomas Guppy at the helm. The goal was to run a regular sailing service from Britain to America.

This was the rainbow's end for Brunel's dream of London-to-New York transatlantic travel. It was the equivalent of a trip on the Orient Express, except that the largest part of the journey would be at sea.

The company's first ship, the 2,300-ton *SS Great Western*, made its maiden voyage in 1838, sailing from Bristol to New York. It took 16 days, longer than a competitor's voyage, but had burned less fuel. As it happened, a rival, the Transatlantic Ship Company, had sent its ship, the *SS Sirius*, across the Atlantic. That ship was the first to make that journey and arrived faster than the *Great Western.* The latter, however, made the return journey in just 14 days, easily outclassing the return journey time of the *Sirius*. Brunel's ship was not technically first in making the journey or recording the first fastest time, but it had won the race that mattered.

Regular service ensued, and Brunel and the rest of the company's directors and investors made a lot of money. They surely looked forward to yearly profits growing by leaps and bounds.

The *Great Western* was a success, yes, but Brunel wanted more. For a start, this first ship had a paddle wheel. Granted, every other large ship of the time had one to power its travel, but Brunel was always pushing the envelope. He wanted nothing short of a cataclysmic thunderstroke in construction: an iron-hulled steamer larger than anyone had ever dreamed of building.

The revolutions in construction and production that were part and parcel of the Industrial Revolution had begat advances in iron production and nascent improvements in steel production. Could those advances be harnessed in the name of shipbuilding?

"When I have formed a decided opinion, no fear of the consequences ever prevents my expressing it."
–Isambard Kingdom Brunel

Brunel had had successes already, many of them, as had his father before him. By this time, both were famous across Britain, across the world. But what of this new design? Was it even possible? How much would it cost? Doggedly, characteristically, Brunel ploughed ahead. He eventually got what he wanted, revolutionising sea travel in the process. The cost, however, was incred ibly high.

Chapter 7

THE SHIP THAT CHANGED THE INDUSTRY

The *SS Great Western* was a success by many measures: It made money, it did what its creators had set out to do, it made a name for the company and its directors and workers, and it showed the promise of oceangoing vessels as more than just vehicles of exploration and trade. Flush with that success, the ship's brainchild, Isambard Kingdom Brunel, launched his next project, the successor ship.

By this time, Brunel was famous in the United Kingdom and elsewhere. He had assisted his father in solving the thorny dilemmas inherent in building the Thames Tunnel; he had bulled his way through the construction of the Box Tunnel on his Great Western Railway line; he had himself designed stations, buildings, bridges, and all manner of other elements associated with that railway line, and he had even designed dockyards in the name of shipbuilding.

Instantly recognisable in his ever-present garb and smoke, Brunel strode the world stage like a man possessed. He was ready for the next challenge. He had bigger dreams of faster and more lucrative voyages.

The original plan was for another ship similar to the *SS Great Western*. Because the destination would again be New York, Brunel planned another paddle-driven wooden ship named *SS City of New York*. However, time and chance played into his hands and altered the course of shipbuilding forever.

His friend and fellow engineer Thomas Guppy ran the Western Ship Company, which owned the *SS Great Western* and sent it across the Atlantic in 1838.

Although Brunel's name was the most famous associated with that company and that voyage, Guppy's was the expertise that Brunel had counted on heavily in constructing and promoting the ship itself. Two other associates, Christopher Claxton and William Patterson, were also involved in the details of the great ship. The latter was another fellow engineer who understood Brunel and his vision; the former was another thing altogether, a Navy veteran and later politician who was also an engineer and was entranced by all things iron.

As if by chance, the men were in Bristol in 1838, after their success with the transatlantic voyage, and witnessed the arrival of a small ship, *Rainbow*, which had an iron hull. It was the product of the well-known engineer Jonathan Laird, who was in the habit of building ships for other countries. The *Rainbow* was a 213-foot packet ship designed for piloting along rivers and canals and sometimes along coastlines, and it was heading back to Antwerp. Intrigued, Claxton and Patterson jumped aboard for the trip. They reported that the iron hull was just the ticket for further advancement. An elated Brunel agreed to convince his board of directors that the *City of New York* should have an iron hull, a very large one. It would be history.

Wood had been the material of choice for ships for a long time. Wooden ships had carried ancient peoples across, up, and down rivers and along coastlines.

"Any part I have taken in examining into the system has been purely from the desire which I always feel to forward good inventions."
–Isambard Kingdom Brunel

The ships that powered the Age of Exploration and consequent eras of conquest were made almost exclusively of wood. Trees were still plentiful, but making wooden ships was getting more expensive, as were many other things during this time. By contrast, the production of iron, thanks to Industrial Revolution innovations, was becoming less expensive. Too, iron proved a barrier against dry rot, barnacles, and other nature-created obstacles to a wooden ship's progress on the high seas.

Another thing that convinced Burnel to go hard into selling an iron hull to his board of directors was the sheer capacity that an iron hull could hold. Iron and its newer cousin, steel, could handle a much heavier load than could wood, so the promise was there to build bigger and heavier ships which would still be safe in the water at any distance.

It was a compelling combination of benefits and would have made a compelling argument. Brunel insisted mightily that his way was the right away – again – and he got his way.

Innovations often take time to manifest and complete, and so it was with the production of Brunel's iron-hulled ship. He wanted it large, larger than ever before. He wanted it to be the best, to keep his investors happy. He wanted all of the bells and whistles. So, in characteristic fashion, he appointed himself chief designer.

His father, Marc Brunel, had a history of grand ambitions achieved through time and error. Marc Brunel's son, Isambard, was no different. The same tenacity that had driven the younger Brunel to survey every inch of the

Great Western Railway line himself compelled him to oversee every bit of the design of the new iron-hulled ship. This, of course, took time.

It was several years between the launches of the first ship, the *SS Great Western*, and the new ship. Both Brunels had come along at a time in history when technology was expanding rapidly and allowed for such grand designs as the two men had to be brought into being. Such was the case with this new ship. But it wasn't just one big new thing that the new ship would incorporate before it launched. It was several innovations employed at once.

As design and production continued in 1840, technology caught up with Brunel again. Into the port of Bristol came the first screw-propelled steamship, the *SS Archimedes* (so named, no doubt, because the ancient Greek inventor had crafted a device

he called the Screw of Archimedes to help with agricultural production). Brunel had decided not to abandon the paddlewheel but was looking for ways to boost its performance. In the screw propeller, he found his improvement in the form of a replacement.

Brunel, for this new giant ship, had decided on again using paddle wheels and needed large metal drive shafts to power them. He had even asked the supplier of his metal tools to invent something; thus, James Nasmyth invented the steel hammer in 1839. After Brunel saw the potential of screw propulsion, however, it was all he could think about in terms of powering his new behemoth of a ship.

Scrapping the paddlewheels in his design, Brunel returned to the drawing board and convinced his board of directors again to back him in this new direction with more time and money. Switching to screw propulsion, he argued, was worth it because it was cheaper and smaller (which should have satisfied the pence-pinchers in the crowd, who would have seen the potential for more cargo onboard) and because it served as a method of stabilisation by virtue of it being placed lower in the ship's hull, giving the watercraft a lower sense of gravity and a means of evening the flow of progress – eliminating the choppy feeling of being onboard as a paddlewheel went in and out of the water. The largest of the six propellers was 15 feet 6 inches across. Again, Brunel argued forcefully for change. Again, he won the day. Production continued.

The board of directors and investors might have lost their patience and thought their investments were lost by the time of the launch, which occurred in July 1843. Prince Albert, consort to Queen Victoria, was on hand to give the royal blessing, having taken the royal train by London, unsurprisingly travelling the Great

Western Railway line. (Unable to resist, Brunel went to London and acted as conductor of the train journey back to Bristol.)

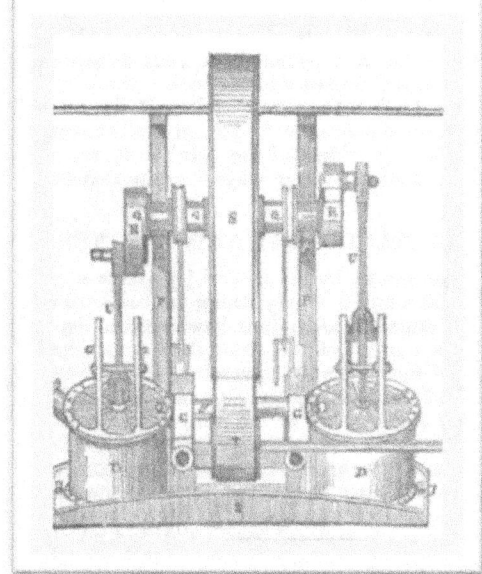

It was a bit of a non-event in the end because Brunel's last-minute additions to the ship made it too big for the existing lock so the ship couldn't leave the harbour. Brunel had to negotiate with another set of people. The Bristol Dock Board and the ship waited for more than a year. A second float-out, in December 1844, hit another technological snag, and the whole thing dragged on even more.

But what a ship! It was 322 feet long, more than a third longer than any steamship built. Its displacement was also significantly larger, by a factor of three than any similar ship up to that point. The ship was 51 feet across at its widest.

The giant beam stretched 50 feet 6 inches. Four decks accommodated a crew of 120, and the passenger capacity was 360. The ship could also carry 1,200 tons of cargo and the same amount of coal for fuel. The six masts were designed to accommodate the less-than-usual number of sails, deemed unneeded with the new screw propulsion system.

Iron abounded: The masts were made of iron, as were the joints with which those masts were fastened to the deck. The rigging was not the usual rope or hemp but iron cable. Iron, as well, was the railing that replaced the usual heavy bulwarks. Five bulkheads were made of iron. Most significantly made of iron was the hull. Inch-thick iron keel plates and iron girders worked together to protect the ship from nature's harm, with the keels overlapping to form a kind of double skin layer, at least in parts. In all, 1,500 tons of iron adorned the ship.

The two powerful steam-driven engines generated 1,600 horsepower, a number unheard of at that time. The main propeller shaft was 68 feet long and 28 inches in diameter. It and two other large shafts housed the six-propeller system, a creation of Brunel's that he called a "windmill" because it looked like one.

Inside was just as large and many times as glamorous. Passengers had the run of the upper two decks; the lower deck was reserved for cargo. Adding to the total content was a pair of broad iron staircases, one at each end of the giant principal saloon, itself 110 feet long and 48 feet wide. Doors from the passenger berths emptied into the saloon to access the other areas of

the ship, including a very large dining area below. The dining saloon was nearly as long as the principal saloon, totalling 98 feet 6 inches long and 30 feet wide.

The dining area was large enough to accommodate tables and chairs to seat 360 people simultaneously. The dining saloon was adorned with 24 white and gold columns, eight pilasters decked out with designs of birds and flowers, and enough mirrors on the walls for everyone to see their reflection at all times.

All those refinements, machinery, and elegance added to a total construction price of £117,000. The original budget was £70,000. It was an enormous cost overrun, even in the heady days of Industrial Revolution construction. But Brunel had instilled confidence in his abilities through his previous successes, and the voyages of the *SS Great Western* were still making the company money. He could still convince others to give him more money, so the expenses were paid, the ship was constructed, and delays were overcome.

"I have found that there is not a single substance we have to deal with, from cast-iron to clay, which should not practically be treated strictly as a yielding elastic substance."
–Isambard Kingdom Brunel

Finally, on July 26, 1845, the *SS Great Britain* set off on its maiden voyage. (By then, the *SS Great Western* had completed nearly 70 transatlantic voyages.) It had taken seven years between ship buildings, but the wait was worth it for many. Brunel was elated.

The captain of this first voyage was not Claxton, Brunel's longtime collaborator, but James Hosken, another Navy veteran of the Napoleonic Wars who had also captained the *SS Great*

Western. The trip took 14 days, 21 hours, nowhere near the record for such a voyage. However, the ship was larger than any that had ever embarked on such a journey. It was history in the sailing. It was the first iron-hulled ship of its size anywhere in the world, and it sailed across the Atlantic without having to refuel or even imagine doing so. Meanwhile, Hosken improved the travel time slightly on the way back, returning home in 13½ days.

Such an achievement would elate many people and send some over the moon. Perfectionists rarely settle, however. Not satisfied, always thinking of new things to try, Brunel went to work again, improving the design by adding more iron to each propeller of the six blades. It worked, making the journey quicker; however, the second voyage of the *SS Great Britain*, like many ships before and since, ran into weather problems and lost three of those propeller blades, along with one of the masts. The 104 passengers aboard (59 more than on the maiden voyage) would have had a rough time but would not have been surprised. Such was common in those days, and workers repaired it all.

Also, during this time, it was all too common for ships to run aground. Even with the most advanced technologies yet invented, ships encountered difficulties they couldn't avoid. Such was the case on that second voyage, in October 1845, when the *SS Great Britain* ran aground off the coast of Massachusetts in America. With less than three dozen passengers onboard for the return journey, the ship again encountered difficulty, losing four propellers during the rough crossing. However, it had made the journey in 13 days, a new record.

One of Brunel's innovations was causing problems because the ship rolled in calm weather due to the lack of many sails. The famed engineer must have thought this a bit of historical irony. Still, he set about making it all work, again securing funding from investors after promising more and more profits ahead. To the propeller system, he went trimming, removing two of the six and reverting to four, which had been the suggestion of his fellow engineer Francis Pettit Smith, architect of the *SS Archimedes*. It was a rare instance of admitting that someone else had been right, but Brunel was pragmatic to recognise what needed doing, regardless of who had come up with the idea in the first place. Shaving off more of the iron, Brunel removed the third mast and converted the iron rigging to the usual consistency. In a nod to existing technology, he added a pair of very large bilge keels to either side to help stabilise during calm. Thus, reprovisioned and significantly augmented, the *SS Great Britain* was done for 1845, home for the winter, awaiting more voyages in the warmer months of the following year.

That year began with a bang, as the mighty ship finished two round trips to New York with flying colours. Such a voyage, considered as dangerous or time-consuming as they come, was beginning to seem commonplace. However, it was still a long journey in both directions, and even the most well-designed ship could face problems. Only after the ship was docked back in Bristol did workers discover that repairs were needed to a chain drum.

The fifth voyage of the *SS Great Britain* was the last ever made for Brunel's company. Of course, Brunel and his friends and investors had no way of knowing this. They were making plans for many more transatlantic voyages, and Brunel was also in hot pursuit of a contract to deliver mail on such journeys. The experienced James Hosken was again at the wheel, and the route would have been familiar. On September 22, 1846, the ship had not gone far, running aground in Dundrum Bay, Ireland. A combination of bad weather and incorrect calculations based on out-of-date charts led the ship to its rocky destination.

Languishing for nearly a year, the ship fell victim to rough waters and lost much of its timber. A desperate Brunel designed a wooden shield to protect the remainder of the ship from the waves and then moved on to other things. The ship finally found water again in August 1847, only to be taken back to Liverpool and abandoned, at least by Brunel's company. As monumental as the ship's achievements were, the ship was still an asset in a business and an asset, at that, that was no longer producing and appeared to be unable to do so again anytime soon. Gibbs, Bright & Co., which once had represented the Western Shipping Company, bought the *SS Great Britain* for a relative song, £25,000 – less than it took to get the ship off the shoals in Ireland.

The new owners made all needed repairs, keeping the ship as it was, and then returned it to its passenger liner service. They regularly went across the Atlantic and back, adding an upper deck to double the number of passengers. The huge difference at this point was that the starting point for these journeys was Liverpool and, with the exception of the first such voyage (which took the expected route to New York City), the destination was Melbourne, in far-away Australia. As it happened, the restored ship made many a journey Down Under, taking many fortune-chasers to the newly discovered gold fields and thousands of people moving to their new homes. The ship had surely designed for long voyages, and Brunel no doubt would have been pleased to know that such was possible and being done.

The *SS Great Britain,* once referred to by a British newspaper as "the greatest experiment since Creation," thus passed its remaining days doing runs to and from Down Under. The one stint that was different during this period was time spent sailing for the British Navy during the Crimean War in the 1850s. By the 1870s, the main purpose of the once grand apple in the eye of Brunel's dreams was hauling coal from Wales to the American West Coast.

The last voyage of the fabled ship was in 1886 when it ran aground off the Falkland Islands. There it stayed, serving as a coal and wool store for other ships for five decades. Determined sailors scuttled the ship in 1936. All was not lost, however. Eventually, the giant ship would make one more voyage – home.

Chapter 8

MEASURING PROGRESS

The *SS Great Britain* revolutionised the shipping industry. Never before had a steamship combined an iron hull with screw propulsion. The successful voyages of the mighty ship proved possible what Brunel had known but still had to prove by doing. In very short order, competitors arose.

One of the main rivals was the Cunard Line, which began in 1840. Brunel desperately wanted to win a contract to deliver mail from the U.K. Government to the United States. Still, it was Cunard, named after owner and ship magnate Samuel Cunard, who was eventually awarded the contract. The RMS *Britannia* was the first of that company's line to carry Royal Mail via steamship across the Atlantic Ocean.

Quickly expanding, Cunard built more ships and sailed more times. This contract put the company in the perfect position to be called on to build ships for service in the Crimean War, which began in 1853. Cunard would eventually supply ships to other countries' governments and, inevitably, build larger and larger ships, creating some of the world's most well-known giant passenger ships, including, in the early 20th Century, the *Carpathia*, which rescued survivors of the ill-fated *Titanic*, and the *Lusitania*, sunk during World War I.

More recent products of the Cunard company and its subsidiaries or partners include the *Queen Elizabeth 2*, a mammoth cruise ship that once sailed the world's oceans but now acts as a floating hotel in the Middle East.

Across the ocean, the Americans were catching up. The *SS California*, sailing for the Pacific Mail Steamship Company, launched in 1848, embarking on regular routes into the Pacific Ocean and taking mail, freight, and passengers from Panama to the West Coast of America.

Such a journey would eventually be expanded to include sailing from America's East Coast to its West Coast, around the southern tip of South America, and a desire to cut down the length of that journey would eventually provide the impetus for building the Panama Canal, the various locks of which many a steamship would traverse.

Brunel wasn't done, however. He had bigger dreams still. Always looking ahead, always planning in bold strokes, confident in his own abilities to overcome problems and convince others to see his point of view, he set his sights on a bigger ship still, combining the prowess of the *Great Western* and the promise of the *Great Britain*. As did many people then, he turned his gaze eastward, settling on constructing a ship that could sail to India and the East without the hassle or hindrance of stopping to reload coal. The British had been in India with purpose since 1601 and the formation of the East India Company. By Brunel's time, British factories in India were humming, churning out goods that would be sent to Britain and the rest of Europe on land and by sea. The desire was always there for more.

Thus, Brunel's greatest achievement was born, the *Great Eastern*. It was more of the same and yet more of everything: more iron, more power, more passenger room, more cargo space, more potential for farther and faster journeys.

All the elements of the *Great Britain* were there: the iron hull, the screw propulsion, and the massive internal iron machinery. It was all on a bigger scale. In fact, the original name for this new ship was *Leviathan*, after the name of a mythical giant monster.

The *Great Britain* was more than 300 feet long. Brunel's design for the new ship had it at 600 feet long. That kind of expansion in size would necessitate a compromise, he finally decided. Rather than depend solely on screw propulsion, building twin propeller systems to power the

giant watercraft, he combined old with new, employing his second ship's propeller system and his first ship's paddlewheel (with, of course, the obligatory sail system, across six masts, for backup). The propeller (still with four blades) was 23 feet 11 inches across. The diameter of the twin paddlewheels was 55 feet 9 inches. A total of five engines (four for the wheels) powered the giant ship, generating 8,000 horsepower.

Unsurprisingly, the interior was larger than the *Great Britain* as well. A potential passenger complement necessitated one very large dining saloon, for starters; as well, the interior includes a larger number of passenger berths. The opulence on display was without compare.

Regarding the exterior, depending yet again on wrought iron (because steel was still too experimental at this stage), Brunel improved his overlay approach to *Great Britain*'s hull and made the *Great Eastern* hull a full double skin. This required, in all, 30,000 iron plates.

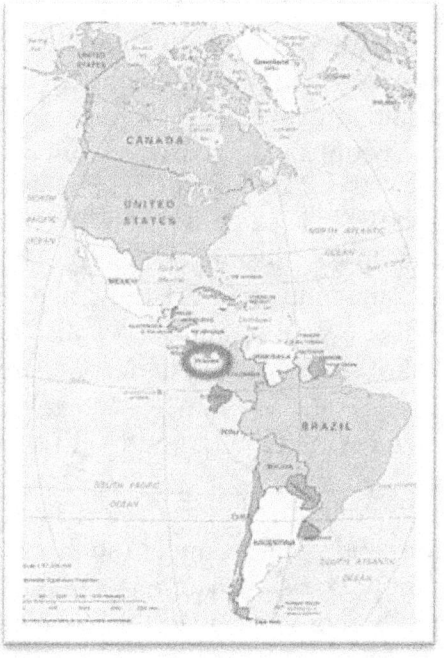

The keel was laid down in 1854. However, as with previous projects, Brunel had to wait for his vision to come true because of cost overruns and the need to invent new ways of doing things. He and his team finally achieved the first float-out on November 3, 1857 – of a sort. The ship stalled on the launch rails; efforts to get it going resulted in the deaths of a few workers and injuries to others. Brunel went back to work, future-proofing, and set a new date of January 30 the following year. Many observers would have been forgiven for abandoning him and his stubbornness, deployed often enough in the face of bad luck or subpar planning. However, it was all still on, and enough of his investors and friends trusted him and his track record enough to let him carry on. And so, he did, and he found a way through again.

Again thwarted, this time by very high winds, Brunel delayed the launch by a day. He had gamed the system by employing a system of chains and windlasses and a healthy dose of machinery to help coax the ship down in the water. It all worked to perfection on January 31, 1858.

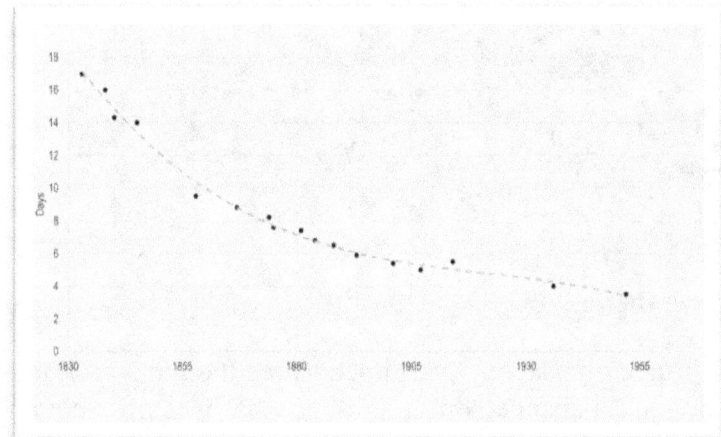

That was the launch, however. The fitout remained, which took another eight months and required another cash infusion of hundreds of thousands of pounds. As big as Brunel's dreams and visions were, they invariably brought very large price tags.

As it happened, Brunel went through three shipping companies, getting the *Great Eastern* from design to maiden voyage. He achieved that goal, at long last, on June 17, 1860. The giant ship crossed New York without incident, adding to Brunel's legacy. The giant ship had a passenger capacity of 4,000, which would not be surpassed for another 60 years. Sadly, he was not there to see it, having died the year before.

His dream lived on, however. Iron hulls on steamships were becoming commonplace, as was self-contained transatlantic travel. Following in his footsteps were other inventors and innovators, such as Alfred Holt, whose engine designs improved fuel efficiency, and A.C. Kirk, who designed the triple expansion engine.

This last was the highest step on the ladder to the advent of the ocean liner, which began in the late 19th Century. Ships like the RMS *Oceanic*, which launched the career of the White Star Line, were certainly smaller than the *Great Eastern* but were designed for the long haul and, in particular, exclusively for passenger travel. They had innovations of their own, allowing many more people and things to be onboard.

By the 1880s, shipbuilders were using steel, thanks to improvements in the production process of the most dynamic of metals. The Bessemer Process, finally refined, was in full use by this time, and industries left, right, and centre were spending money hand over fist to take advantage of this new metal and its promise and potential. Ships at sea would never be the same, as the level of safety of the people onboard those ships was significantly improved.

Transatlantic Crossing Times 1833 – 1952

They would be bigger, faster, stronger, and capable of great feats. They would carry people, goods and weapons and, in some cases, function as weapons of war. Along the way, coal-fuelled steam power switched to steam turbine engines. Then diesel engines, the ultimate extension of today's most advanced fuel, nuclear power, which can be seen making aircraft carriers and submarines go even now.

What didn't disappear was the presence of iron and its successor steel in the list of ship construction materials. Brunel's vision – of a ship made of wrought iron that was big enough to sail across the Atlantic – came true in his lifetime. In his quest for something bigger and better, he achieved some of his goals; however, fulfilling his ultimate vision needed newer technology for the vision to become reality. Such was the case with many visionaries: They saw the future and worked toward it but didn't always get there.

The design, building, and successful sailing of massive ocean liners, dreadnoughts and other giant ships of war fulfilled one man's dogged insistence on imagining what was possible and then setting out to see if he could make it happen.

One benefit for the world's trees due to the ongoing decision to make ship hulls out of iron, and not wood was a drop in the rate of deforestation. This is still a problem today, as has been well documented in recent years. However, the reduction rate in the world's tree population was still increasing rapidly throughout the Age of Exploration. As the need for more ships created, the need for more trees felled to harvest more wood to build those ships. The move away from wood, at least for ship's hulls, allowed natural tree repopulation to retake a position of sorts. In more recent times, concerted efforts to plant more trees have also helped in this regard.

Still of more benefit was the reuse of iron and steel in new ships. The metallic nature of these new materials makes them malleable in a way that wood is not, enabling recycling of parts of damaged ships as elements of repair or even in new construction. Such is the concept of sustainability seen in using and reusing metals in a way that wasn't possible on such a scale when the material of choice was good old wood.

A large part of the shipping in the late 19th Century and early 20th Century was passenger liners taking people to America. A great migration of displaced people and those otherwise yearning for better opportunities in life boarded giant ships in Europe and disembarked in New York, there to disperse perhaps into the country's interior. Such was the main duty of the successor ships to Brunel's iron-hulled behemoths. The Cunard Line and the White Star Line were prime movers in this area, churning out ever larger ships designed to move people and cargo across the Atlantic, primarily, but also other giant waterways.

The 19th Century had no shortage of wars. The United States and the United Kingdom fought in 1812–1814. A whole fleet of British troops crossed the Atlantic to prosecute that war at a time when the Napoleonic Wars were winding down. The relative lack of wars enabled Brunel and his ilk to pursue their technological advances in peace. However, the Crimean War flared up in the middle of the century, and the American Civil War began not long after the launch of the *Great Eastern*.

As the 19th century drew to a close, the focus was more on passenger and freight shipbuilding, but ships of war were never far from the minds of governments. The U.K. fought a war in South

Africa as the 19th Century became the 20th. The Great War consumed the attention of seemingly the world in 1914–1918. The Spanish Civil War captured the attention of a great many in 1936–1939. Another cataclysm, World War II, was on the heels of that internecine conflict. Conflicts in Korea and Vietnam followed not long afterwards.

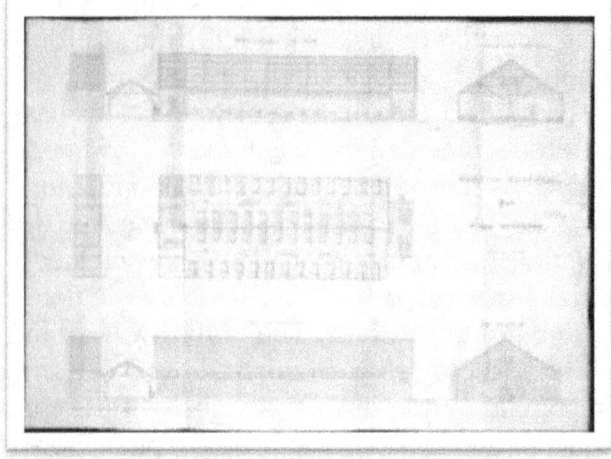

All of those wars involved shipping and shipbuilding to some degree. More and more ships of war had iron and, later, steel hulls and parts. The drive for better, faster, stronger, and lighter consumed war planners in nations around the globe. Many of those ships had guns, some were seaborne mini airfields, and many were transport ships – for men and materiel in the war effort and food, clothing, and medicine. First, the dreadnought and then the battleship replaced the ship of the line, both latter behemoths boasting protective sheathing that would have made Brunel proud.

The switch to iron and steel also enabled ships to go on longer trade routes to inhospitable climates – no more worrying about how ice floes would affect the ship's hull. Exploration, certainly, but even more so, trade expanded rapidly and internationally. Only the aeroplane could achieve more in terms of shortening the time between destinations.

In the same way, the shipbuilders of modern times have employed strategies in chemistry and physics to make modern iron and steel ships more resistant to the harsh conditions of the world's oceans, following in the footsteps of the Industrial Revolution inventors and then Brunel and his ilk in the switch from coal to steam and from wood to iron. Travel by sea is especially hard on a ship's hull, no matter how innovative the surface material or design is; scientists are always looking for ways to reduce corrosion. Some things don't change.

Today's ships, sleek and sharp and very large and fast, owe much of their interior and exterior design to Brunel and his vision. To him goes the credit for creating the first modern ship, the *SS Great Britain*. Many ships built after this could trace their lineage to the great man and his ideas.

Afterword: The End of the Line

Isambard Kingdom Brunel had the vision and imagination to pursue dreams bigger than himself. His contributions to the future, not only of the United Kingdom but also to humanity, are legion. His bold style had many fans and many detractors. His failures were some, his successes more. He is perhaps most well-known for his work in the railway and shipping industries. He was legendary for his ability to convince other people to give him their money to achieve a joint vision of improvement and technological advancement. However, he did extend his considerable expertise to other things. He was adept at designing buildings, as evidenced by the still-standing and well-photographed Paddington Station. At the height of the Crimean War, in 1855, Brunel designed for his government a prefabricated hospital that could be shipped to the front.

He and his team took only five months to design and build what became the Renkioi Hospital, which was then shipped to Scutari, near where the famous Florence Nightingale was working. Brunel's designs incorporated all manner of hygienic protections, a major improvement on existing medical conditions.

He also suggested a design for a floating gun battery to assist in besieging Russian ports like the famed Sebastapol. The Government passed on that one.

Back in the shipyards, he was on the dock of his beloved *Great Eastern* on September 5, 1859. In the months between float-out and maiden voyage, he suffered a stroke. He did not recover and died ten days later.

Monuments and testaments to him abound. His statues dot the landscape, as do things (streets, universities) named after him.

His legacy is long and somewhat complicated. He is still clearly remembered for his accomplishments. As recently as 2001, a BBC poll sought to collate the 10 Greatest Britons. Perhaps unsurprisingly, World War II-era Prime Minister Winston Churchill topped the poll given relatively recent events. Brunel was second. Many bridges that he designed and built are still in use.

Most famously, perhaps, is something that isn't a bridge, the Thames Tunnel, which he designed and built with his father. The famous underground passageway spent several years as a walkway and then a roadway but is now part of the London Underground.

At nearby Rotherhithe, the one-time Brunel Engine House is now the Brunel Museum. And his world-changing ship, the *SS Great Britain*, is again on display at a museum in his beloved Bristol.

The *SS Great Britain* revolutionised the shipping industry, laying the groundwork for much of what came later. Although Brunel designed this ship in the 1830s, and it made its maiden voyage a decade later, the ship is still with us in the form of a restoration.

With Brunel dead, the legacy of the great ship was intact, but its purpose had changed. Its new owners turned their sights southward and began journeys to Australia. A gold rush in the 1850s attracted untold numbers of immigrants, and the *Great Britain* took thousands of such travellers on a long journey from one homeland to a new one. Stories told by these passengers abound. Some saw porpoises and sharks and whales. Travellers on one voyage in 1865 witnessed a total lunar eclipse. A few hundred passengers were onboard in 1872 when the *Great Britain* crew rescued the crew of another ship that had been abandoned in the Atlantic Ocean.

It wasn't just human passengers, either. Because the journey from the U.K. to Australia could take up to two months, taking meat to last the entire trip wasn't an option because refrigeration to accommodate such a practice hadn't been adopted yet. Even with the best of salt and other preservatives, meat at that time would spoil during such a long period onboard a ship. The solution was to take live animals, which were then used for food. A voyage in 1859 was recorded as having, among the animal passengers, more than 100 live sheep, three dozen pigs, more than 300 ducks, 400 geese, 30 turkeys, and a cow.

Among the remembrances is this from a passenger named J.J. Hardwick, who, during a voyage in 1852, wrote this in his diary:

> "... dinner which was first rate, quite such as you would get at the best hotels: soup, grouse, pigeon, and vel pies, pork, ham and other meat dishes, sundry puddings and targs and jelly, blancmange, cheese, celery and after all a dessert."

The ship made the return journey, sailing back to Liverpool, often with many passengers onboard. A Swiss businessman, Herman Zumstein, had moved to Australia in the 1850s and, in 1863, was travelling to his home country to visit family. His diary entry from May 10, 1863, served as a reminder that sea journeys could be very rough and tumble:

> "Got up with a nasty cold. Heavy gale from the west, rain and spray. Divine service in the cuddy. Confined within the whole day on account of the weather. All hands psalms and hymns the livelong day. The whole ship and all over plunging and rolling like mad. Not a dry place on the whole ship. In short, everybody moping about as uncomfortably and listlessly as possible."

The passenger journeys eventually ceased and in 1882, the ship became a very large freighter, hauling coal around the Atlantic. On one such journey, in 1886, the fabled iron-hulled craft ran aground off the Falkland Islands. With no Brunel around to save the day, the well-lavished giant ship lost much of its infrastructure to the ravages of time and nature. A nearby company used the ship to store coal for many years, at one point providing fuel for British ships that defeated a German fleet in the World War I Battle of the Falkland Islands.

The once-proud ship served as a source of metal for U.K. ships during World War II. And the languishing continued. Eventually, interest in the ship renewed, and a collection of donations by some famous people funded a salvage operation.

Restorers discovered a large crack in the hull and, worried that it would split further on the journey, asked local people to contribute old mattresses to help fill the void. The masts were also deemed a risk, so a local carpenter was found to cut them off. Even the fabled iron hull had holes after so many years, so restorers found ways to patch those well before transport could occur. In a decision that would have made Brunel smile, one of the engineers ordered steel plates to be put on top and bottom of the giant crack in the hull to keep it from growing.

After the ship was successfully moved onto a pontoon, it was towed back to Bristol and then lovingly restored. At one point during the journey up the River Avon, Brunel's most famous ship was towed under his famous bridge, making for a wonderful photo opportunity. After extensive and painstaking recovery work, the ship was relaunched in 2005, this time as a museum. Hundreds of thousands of people visit each year.

The *SS Great Eastern* carried on without Brunel. Its maiden voyage, June 17, 1860, occurred after his death. The crew on that 11-day voyage to New York was much larger than the passenger list, but the ship arrived safely and received quite an enthusiastic reaction, as had the *Great Britain* a few years earlier. The great ship took a bit of a detour on the way home, stopping off in a few American ports and even welcoming a visit from then-U.S. President James Buchanan. All of that did little to offset the huge costs incurred by the journey compared to the little revenue from the paltry number of passengers. The next journey involved carrying freight, which did pay its way after revenues were collected on the other end.

Voyage times kept going down and down. A trip in 1860 took only eight days and 6 hours. That was all well and good as long as the weather was favourable. Even as big and mighty as the *Great Eastern* was, it wasn't immune to the ravages of the bad-weather sea. A huge hurricane in September 1861 did damage that would have ruined a smaller ship, ripping off both paddlewheels, mangling the rudder beyond repair, and taking away the entire sails. Left only with the screw propeller, the ship limped homeward and arrived without further incident.

The ship's owners wanted to maintain their reputation as carrying only the highest level of society as passengers. So, although they agreed to haul all freight, they refused to take any immigrants bound for the United States onboard. As such, the ship's fortunes continued to be in doubt.

The situation was compounded by a run-in with a large set of rocks in August 1862. Even Brunel's famous double-skin iron hull was not immune to tearing from sharp-edge rocks at high speed, and so at what was later named Great Eastern Rock, it was that the ship struck hard enough to tear a 9-foot-wide and 83-foot-long hole in the hull. The outer hull was strong enough that the tear didn't reach the inner hull, but the ship was still damaged and needed repair. Such was done at great cost. To many of the company directors, the ship's days were numbered.

That was indeed the case, as the company tired of losing money and decided to auction it off. As it happened, the winners at auction were four of the board of directors, who turned around and rented the ship out to an American enterprise laying a replacement telegraph cable under the Atlantic Ocean to connect America and Europe.

Workers had laid the first such cable between 1854 and 1858, and Queen Victoria had sent President James Buchanan a telegraphic message of congratulations. However, the signal quality needed to be improved to meet requirements, and to fix it by increasing the voltage, an engineer rendered the cable unusable. Even though all of that work had been done, the existing cabling was, in effect, dead weight and the only option was to lay a new cable using new and improved materials.

The *Great Eastern* was thus part of one of the 19th Century's greatest communication achievements, carrying at one point nearly 14,000 miles of cable to plunk down under the sea floor. One significant delay occurred in 1865 when workers lost the cable end on the Atlantic floor. They returned the following year and completed the job. The new cabling proved up to the task, and telegraphic communications resumed. Flush with success, the ship's crew accepted another similar job, laying undersea cables in the Indian Ocean.

After these successes, the great ship had a rather ignominious end. Languishing in Milford for 11 years, she escaped only to be sold again and used as an entertainment venue of various sorts and even a floating billboard for a department store.

Her one last hurrah was a trip to Liverpool for the 1886 Exhibition. The following year saw her sold again to a company that used her to get shallow shipwrecks up and floating again. The final sale in 1888 resulted in her being sold off as scrap. The *Great Eastern* survived indelibly in the memories of the people who saw her afloat. The ship exists now only in parts. The top mast still is a flag pole on the grounds of the Liverpool Football Club. Other significant interior parts are known to be in museums and private collections. This largest of Brunel's ships met the same fate as his first, the scrap heap. It was not what he would have wanted.

APPENDIX

THE WORLD'S LARGEST
PASSENGER SHIPS: 19TH CENTURY

Year	Ship Name	Length, Passengers
1831	*SS Royal William*	160 feet 155 passengers
1837	*SS Great Western*	252 feet 128 passengers
1839	*SS British Queen*	245 feet 207 passengers
1843	*SS Great Britain*	321 feet 360 passengers
1853	*SS Atrato*	350 feet 760+ passengers
1858	*SS Great Eastern*	692 feet 4,000 passengers
1888	*SS City of New York*	560 feet 1,740 passengers
1893	RMS *Campania* RMS *Lucania*	622 feet 2,000 passengers
1897	*Kaiser Wilhelm der Grosse*	655 feet 1,506 passengers
1899	RMS *Oceanic*	704 feet 1,710 passengers

THE WORLD'S LARGEST PASSENGER SHIPS: 20TH CENTURY

Year	Ship Name	Length, Passengers
1901	RMS *Celtic*	701 feet 2,857 passengers
1903	RMS *Cedric*	700 feet 1,223 passengers
1904	RMS *Baltic*	729 feet 2,875 passengers
1906	SS *Kaiserin Auguste Victoria*	243 feet 110 passengers
1907	RMS *Lusitania*	787 feet 2,198 passengers
1907	RMS *Mauretania*	790 feet 2,165 passengers
1911	RMS *Olympic*	882 feet 2,435 passengers
1912	RMS *Titanic*	883 feet 2,435 passengers
1913	SS *Imperator*	906 feet 4,234 passengers
1922	RMS *Majestic*	956 feet 2,145 passengers
1935	SS *Normandie*	1,029 feet 1,972 passengers

THE WORLD'S LARGEST PASSENGER SHIPS: 20TH CENTURY

Year	Ship Name	Length, Passengers
1936	RMS *Queen Mary*	1.019 feet 2,139 passengers
1946	RMS *Queen Elizabeth*	1,031 feet 2,283 passengers
1972	*SS France*	1,035 feet 2,044 passengers
1987	MS *Sovereign of the Seas*	880 feet 2,850 passengers
1990	*SS Norway*	1,035 feet 2,565 passengers
1995	*Sun Princess*	857 feet 2,010 passengers
1996	*Carnival Destiny*	893 feet 2,642 passengers
1998	*Grand Princess*	951 feet 2,590 passengers
1999	*Voyager of the Seas*	1,020 feet 3,138 passengers

THE WORLD'S LARGEST
PASSENGER SHIPS: 21ST CENTURY

Year	Ship Name	Length, Passengers
2000	*Explorer of the Seas*	1.020 feet 3,114 passengers
2002	*Navigator of the Seas*	1,020 feet 4,000 passengers
2003	RMS *Queen Mary 2*	1,132 feet 2,620 passengers
2006	*Freedom of the Seas*	1,111 feet 4,515 passengers
2007	*Liberty of the Seas*	1,111 feet 4,960 passengers
2009	*Oasis of the Seas*	1,180 feet 6,780 passengers
2016	*Harmony of the Seas*	1,188 feet 6,780 passengers
2018	*Symphony of the Seas*	1,184 feet 6,680 passengers

THE BRUNEL MUSEUM

Among the thousands of items displayed at the Brunel Museum is a school report from when the precocious lad was 14 and attending the *Institute M Massin* in France. Among the details:

PRIZES AWARDED:

- 1st Prize in Elementary Maths
- Prize of the Semester of the Class of Maths
- Prize of the Semester in French Language, History, and Geography
- 2nd Honourable Mention in Drawing, 2nd Division

SUBJECT REPORTS:

- Religious homework: properly fulfilled
- French language: showed improvement
- Latin language: must improve
- Analysis: Good
- History: Good
- Geography: Good
- Maths: Very Good
- Drawing: Very Good
- German language: Very Good, Diligent
- Health: Good
- Behaviour: Beyond Reproach

Final note: This young man gave all his teachers the fullest satisfaction, providing brilliant expectations for the future.